LET'S FIND OUT ABOUT

Islamic Mosques

Ruqaiyyah Waris Maqsood

www.raintreepublishers.co.uk
Visit our website to find out more information about Raintree books.

To order:
 Phone 44 (0) 1865 888112
📄 Send a fax to 44 (0) 1865 314091
💻 Visit the Raintree Bookshop at www.raintreepublishers.co.uk to browse our catalogue and order online.

First published in Great Britain by Raintree, Halley Court, Jordan Hill, Oxford, OX2 8EJ, part of Harcourt Education.
Raintree is a registered trademark of Harcourt Education Ltd.

© Harcourt Education Ltd 2006.
First published in paperback in 2007.
The moral right of the proprietor has been asserted.

Editorial: Daniel Nunn and Sarah Chappelow
Design: Ron Kamen and Philippa Baile
Picture research: Hannah Taylor and Sally Claxton
Production: Duncan Gilbert
Religious consultant: Toby Mayer

Originated by Modern Age
Printed and bound in China by WKT

ISBN 10: 1 844 21142 8 (hardback)
ISBN 13: 978 1 844 21142 5 (hardback)
09 08 07 06 05
10 9 8 7 6 5 4 3 2 1

ISBN 10: 1 844 21177 0 (paperback)
ISBN 13: 978 1 844 21177 7 (paperback)
11 10 09 08 07 06
10 9 8 7 6 5 4 3 2 1

British Library Cataloguing in Publication Data
Maqsood, Ruqaiyyah Waris
  Let's find out about Islamic mosques
  1. Mosques – Juvenile literature
  2. Islam – Customs and practices – Juvenile literature
  I. Title II. Islamic mosques
  297.6'5
A full catalogue record for this book is available from the British Library.

Acknowledgements
The publishers would like to thank the following for permission to reproduce photographs:

Alamy Images pp. **7** (Image Solutions), **22** (Jeremy Nicholl); Corbis pp. **5 bottom** (Jeremy Horner), **11 top** (Jeremy Horner), **15 bottom** (Sergio Dorantes), **17** (David H. Wells), **20** (Reuters), **21** (Reuters/Ajay Verma), **23** (Sergio Dorantes), **27** (Sygma/J. B. Russell); Getty Images p. **4** (Photodisc); Peter Sanders p. **9 top**; Trip pp. **5 top** (M. Azavedo), **6** (H. Rogers), **8** (H. Rogers), **9 bottom**, **11 bottom** (H. Rogers), **12** (H. Rogers), **13** (H. Rogers), **14**, **15 top** (H. Rogers), **16**, **18** (H. Rogers), **19** (H. Rogers), **24**, **25** (H. Rogers), **26** (H. Rogers).

Cover photograph of the Zawawi Mosque in Muscat, Oman reproduced with permission of Getty Images/Taxi.

Every effort has been made to contact copyright holders of any material reproduced in this book. Any omissions will be rectified in subsequent printings if notice is given to the publishers.

The paper used to print this book comes from sustainable resources.

Contents

Words appearing in the text in bold, **like this**, are explained in the Glossary. The Muslim words used in this book are listed with a pronunciation guide on page 29.

What is a mosque?

A mosque is a place of **worship** for Muslims. Although Muslims can pray anywhere, they prefer to meet somewhere that is clean and peaceful. Prayer is very important to Muslims. There are five special prayers that they say every single day.

But mosques are not just places of worship. Many mosques run special schools called **madrasahs**. These are for people to study **Arabic** and learn more about **Islam**.

Many mosques have domes and tall towers called minarets. The crescent moon symbol at the top of the minaret is the symbol of Islam.

crescent moon

minaret

The Faisal Mosque in Islamabad, Pakistan, is built in the shape of a tent.

Did you know
The Arabic word for *mosque* is *masjid*, which means "place in which to bow down". This is because Muslims bow down when they pray to God.

Mosques are also places for looking after other people. Sometimes people with nowhere to live can sleep in a mosque. They might also be fed there.

These Muslims are resting inside a mosque.

Finally, mosques are places where Muslims can meet together just to have fun and enjoy free time with friends.

Islam and Muslims

Islam means "to submit to the will of God". Muslims must always try to do what God wants. Muslims believe there is only one God, who created everything. The name for God in **Arabic** is **Allah**.

Allah sent messengers, called **prophets**, to tell people how they should live. The last of these prophets was called Muhammad (**pbuh**). Muhammad (pbuh) was born in Makkah, in Arabia. He passed on God's messages for about 23 years, and died in 632 CE. His collection of messages is called the **Qur'an**.

Islam is a worldwide religion. These women are praying at a mosque in London, in the United Kingdom.

Did you know

Muslims always write "pbuh" when they mention Muhammad. It means "Peace be upon him".

During their lives, Muslims must do five special things known as the "Pillars" of Islam. These are:

★ to believe that there is only one God and that Muhammad (pbuh) was His prophet

★ to say a special prayer called the **salah** five times every day

★ to **fast** during the month of **Ramadan**

★ to give money to poor people

★ to make a special religious journey, or **pilgrimage**, to the Ka'bah **shrine** in Makkah. This is called the **Hajj**.

This man is saying one of the five daily prayers.

Mosques great and small

Some mosques are very large, and some are very small. Sometimes mosques are not even buildings at all. A mosque can be a room or even just a special area set aside in the street or in a park.

Some mosques are very famous, such as the Dome of the Rock mosque in Jerusalem, or the Blue Mosque in Istanbul, Turkey. Famous mosques like these are usually beautifully decorated with carpets, tiles, or glass. They often have amazing pillars, domes, and **minarets**.

In Muslim countries such as **Egypt**, there are even places set aside for people to pray in the street.

In countries where there are not very many Muslims, other buildings are often turned into mosques. These can include large family houses or even apartments over shops.

The Great Mosque in Makkah sometimes has more than a million pilgrims inside, visiting the Ka'bah shrine.

This house in the United Kingdom has been turned into a mosque.

Did you know

The most important mosque in the world is at the Ka'bah **shrine** in the city of Makkah, in Saudi Arabia. About two million Muslim **pilgrims** now go there every year on the **Hajj**.

Inside a mosque

The most important part of a mosque is the hall where people pray. Inside the hall, Muslims form lines when they pray together. There are no seats, so **worshippers** kneel or sit on the carpet.

This diagram shows the layout of a typical mosque.

On one wall, there is a special mark or **niche** called the mihrab. The mihrab shows the direction of Makkah. Muslims face this way when they pray. Near the mihrab there is usually a minbar. The minbar is a platform where the **imam** stands. This is so that everyone can see him.

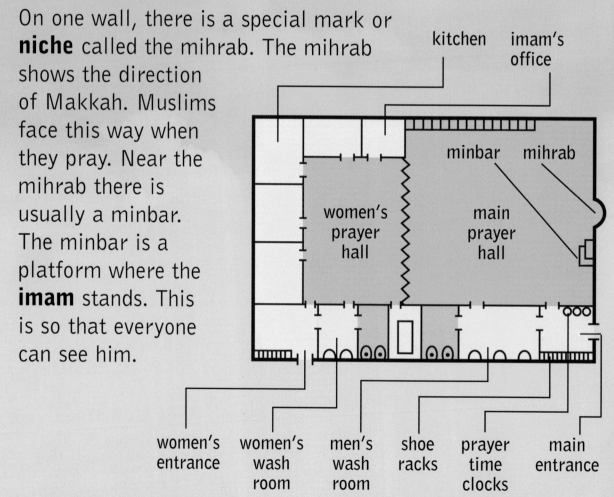

kitchen   imam's office

minbar   mihrab

women's prayer hall

main prayer hall

women's entrance

women's wash room

men's wash room

shoe racks

prayer time clocks

main entrance

A Muslim view

We can talk to **Allah** any time, but our five **salah** prayers are before sunrise, after midday, after the shadows have lengthened, after sunset, and between nightfall and midnight. If we want to pray together at the mosque we have a special timetable.

Hassan, age eight, Morocco

Many mosques have clocks showing the daily prayer times.

In some big mosques, men and women may pray in separate areas and use different entrances. In others, women pray behind the men in the same hall.

Mosque carpets have patterns that help people to stand in a straight line.

mihrab

minbar

Things to see

Mosques often look rather empty compared with other places of **worship**, because there are no pictures or statues. This is because Muslims are taught never to bow down before images. Instead, they should only worship **Allah**.

The Sehzade Mosque in Istanbul, Turkey, is decorated with beautiful wall tiles and Arabic writing.

However, mosques are often decorated with writing of **Arabic** verses from the **Qur'an**. This can be made into beautiful patterns. Many mosques also have stained glass, **chandeliers**, colourful tiles, and carved woodwork.

Sometimes there may be a special Qur'an inside the mosque. This is often kept on a wooden stand called a kursi, so the Qur'an doesn't touch the floor.

This kursi stand is being used to hold a Qur'an in a mosque in Istanbul, Turkey.

A Muslim view

We treat our Qur'ans with great respect. We wash before touching them, and we do not let them touch the floor. When not in use, we cover them up.

Zaynab, age eleven, Iran

Getting ready to worship

Muslims go to **worship** when they hear the call to prayer, or adhan. This is often performed at the top of the mosque's **minaret** by a man called the muezzin.

Worshippers enter mosques quietly and peacefully and treat them with respect. They wear clean clothing in which they can sit on the floor and bow down comfortably. They take off their shoes and leave them outside.

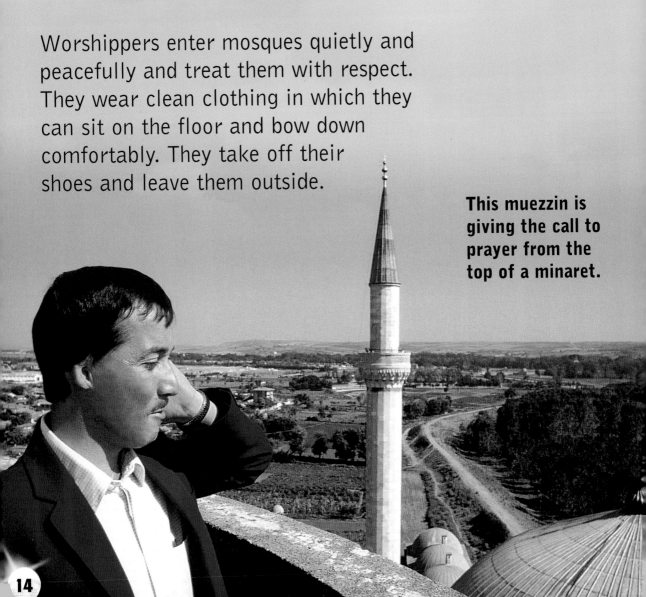

This muezzin is giving the call to prayer from the top of a minaret.

Muslims have a special wash before praying, called **wudu**. They wash their arms, hands, face, mouth, nostrils, ears, head, neck, feet, and ankles. Wudu is a way of showing respect for **Allah**.

Muslim men wash before prayer at a mosque in Delhi, India.

Women cover their heads and bodies from neck to wrist and foot. This covering is called hijab.

> *A Muslim view*
>
> When I pray I put on a special white skirt and veil. This helps me to feel apart from the world and closer to Allah.
> *Noor, age ten, Malaysia*

These women are wearing hijab. They are praying behind the men.

Worshipping at a mosque

These men are performing the salah prayer. When the mosques are full, people have to pray outside.

The **salah** prayer is said five times every day, although not always in a mosque. Everyone says the salah in **Arabic**. It follows a special pattern of lining up, reciting from the **Qur'an**, bowing down, and kneeling on the ground.

On Fridays at midday there is a very special prayer. All male Muslims should go to this if possible. Before it starts, they listen to an **imam** giving a talk. This talk is called a **khutbah**. It might explain something in the Qur'an or be about how something in the news affects Muslims.

In addition to the salah, Muslims often say other prayers throughout the day. These ask **Allah** for help or forgiveness, or thank Him for something good that has happened.

Many Muslims use a special set of beads called subhah to help them concentrate on worshipping Allah.

Ramadan

Ramadan is a very important time for Muslims. For a whole month they get up for a meal before dawn, then have nothing else to eat or drink until sunset. This is called **fasting**. At sunset they have a taste of food and drink to end the day's fast. Then they have a big meal after the evening prayer. Many Muslims take turns to provide free food for anyone who comes to the mosques at this time.

A Muslim view

It's hard to watch non-Muslim friends eating their dinners, especially if they tease us. Also, we get much less sleep. But we do it for Allah's sake, and it makes us strong.

Tariq, age nine, London in the United Kingdom

Members of a Muslim family eat together at their local mosque at the end of a day's fasting during Ramadan.

Every evening, about two hours are spent in extra prayers called tarawih. Over the course of the month, the whole **Qur'an** is recited from start to finish. Some people even spend all of the last ten days of Ramadan praying in the mosque and sleeping there at night.

The most special night is Laylat al-Qadr. This is in memory of when **Allah** sent the first words of the Qur'an. Many Muslims spend all of this night at the mosque.

These British Muslims are saying tarawih prayers at a mosque in London in the United Kingdom.

Festivals and special occasions

Pakistani Muslims pray in the courtyard of the mosque in Karachi during Eid ul-Fitr.

Ramadan ends with a festival called Eid ul-Fitr. Hundreds of Muslims gather for prayers. Sometimes there are too many people to fit into the mosques, so people pray outside instead. In Muslim countries there is a three-day holiday with many parties. Money is collected at the mosque to provide feasts for the poor.

A Muslim view

My favourite day is Eid ul-Fitr because we all get new clothes, pocket-money, and presents, and we have big parties and visit all our friends. *Sarah, age eight, from New York, in the United States*

Eid ul-Adha is a fun time for Muslims. This Indian family is buying balloons to celebrate.

Another festival is Eid ul-Adha, which celebrates the end of the **Hajj**. Every adult provides a whole sheep or goat to feed family and guests, with one-third of the meat sent to the poor. They also visit graveyards to pray for dead loved ones.

Laylat al-Bara'at is two weeks before Ramadan. Many Muslims pray all night in the mosque to ask for **Allah's** forgiveness and think about their future. Some people also hold special celebrations for the birthday of the **Prophet** Muhammad (**pbuh**).

Who works in a mosque?

An imam leads prayers at the Kalyan Mosque in Uzbekistan.

Mosques are busy places. They are run by
an **imam**. Other people help with money,
organization, housing, teaching, and legal
matters. There are also people who work as
carers, cooks, and cleaners.

The imam does not have to work full-time or be
paid, but most imams do get paid. His main jobs
are to lead the prayers, give the **khutbahs**, and
lead the teaching in the special **madrasah** schools.

Imams are respected men with great knowledge of the **Qur'an** and Islamic law. They may advise Muslims on everything from marriage problems to finding work. They should be wise, kind, and honest men.

A Muslim view

I go to madrasah every day for an hour or so after normal school, and at weekends too. It is quite hard, but I am glad to learn **Arabic** and also see my friends.

Abdul Karim, age nine, Nigeria

Imams are not the only people who work in mosques. This teacher is helping students at a madrasah school in Indonesia.

Mosques are important centres for the Muslim **community**. They help Muslims to meet and do things together. At mosques people have fun with others who speak their language and share their beliefs.

Mosques are often used as places for celebration. They are where people hold happy events such as wedding parties or thank-you parties for answered prayers. They are also used to hold funerals, when special prayers are said for those who have died.

This Muslim couple are celebrating their wedding at a mosque in Malaysia.

Bazaars such as this are held to sell Muslim items and to raise money for the local mosque.

Activities at mosques include youth groups, discussion groups and talks, women's groups, and mother and baby clubs. Some mosques even have games and sports facilities. There may also be homework clubs or other classes for people who need extra help with their lives.

Did you know

Mosques offer shelter for visitors or the homeless. Money is raised by holding collections and **bazaars**. There may also be a shop that sells books, clothing, decorations, and other Islamic items.

Worshipping at home

Muslim homes are places of **worship**, too. Families often keep a room or special place clean and ready for prayers. The routine of **wudu** and **salah** is exactly the same whether done at the mosque, at home, at work, or school. Most Muslims also spend time every day in extra prayers and reading the **Qur'an**.

This Muslim family is praying together at home during Ramadan.

Muslim worship also involves behaving respectfully towards **Allah** during daily life. Muslims should not drink alcohol or eat anything made of pork or any meat not killed in a special way called halal. They must also dress respectfully at all times. This usually means covering their bodies from their neck to their ankles.

Many Muslims say *bismillah* (which means "in the name of God") before they start any new activities. This is so they always have "clean" hearts, thoughts, words, and actions.

Did you know

Muslim girls and women often wear clothes that cover their bodies (called hijab) to show respect for Allah. But that does not mean these clothes cannot be beautiful.

Many Muslims spend time reading the Qur'an every day at home.

27

Islam around the world

The religion of **Islam** began in Arabia about 1,400 years ago. Since then, Muslims have travelled all over the world. Today, there are more than one billion Muslims worldwide. Islam is the world's second largest religion, after Christianity. For every 100 people in the world, 20 of them are Muslims.

The greatest numbers of Muslims live in Asia and Africa. There are also large Muslim **communities** in the United States, the United Kingdom, and many other European countries.

Numbers of Muslims around the world (numbers are not exact)

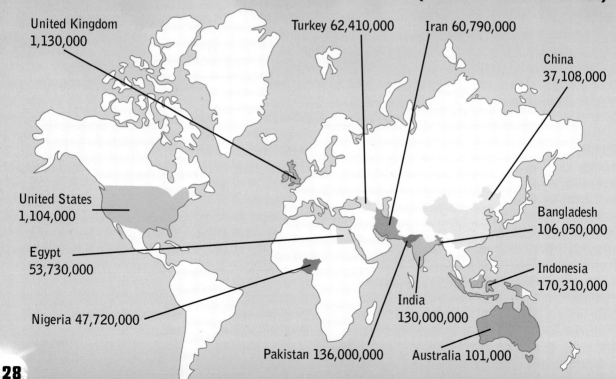

United Kingdom 1,130,000

Turkey 62,410,000

Iran 60,790,000

China 37,108,000

United States 1,104,000

Bangladesh 106,050,000

Egypt 53,730,000

Indonesia 170,310,000

Nigeria 47,720,000

India 130,000,000

Pakistan 136,000,000

Australia 101,000

Muslim words

These are the Muslim words that have been used in this book. You can find out how to say them by reading the pronunciation guide in the brackets after each word.

adhan [ad-thaan] – the call to prayer

Allah [al-laa] – the name for God in Arabic

Eid ul-Adha [eed-ul-ad-haa] – festival held at the end of the Hajj pilgrimage

Eid ul-Fitr [eed ul-fit-er] – festival at the end of Ramadan

hafiz/hafizah [haa-fiz, haa-fiz-aa] – someone who has learned the entire Qur'an by heart

Hajj [hajj] – a special religious journey, or pilgrimage, to Makkah

halal [ha-laal] – a special way of preparing meat, so that Muslims can eat it

hijab [hi-jaab] – modest clothing worn by women that covers the whole body

imam [i-maam] – leader of the prayers at a mosque

Ka'bah [kaa-baa] – the cube-shaped shrine to God in Makkah

khutbah [koot-baa] – a short talk or sermon

kursi [koor-see] – a wooden stand that is used to hold a Qur'an

Laylat al-Bara'at [lie-lat-al-ba-raat] – a night two weeks before Ramadan that many Muslims spend at the mosque

Laylat al-Qadr [lie-lat-al-ka-der] – a night when Muslims remember the first time Allah revealed the Qur'an to the Prophet Muhammad (pbuh)

madrasah [mad-rass-aa] – a mosque school where people can learn more about Islam

mihrab [mi-h-raab] – a niche or marking that shows the direction of Makkah

minbar [min-baar] – platform or steps that an imam stands on so people can see him

muezzin [moo-ad-thin] – the person who makes the call to prayer

Qur'an [koo-raan] – the collection of messages brought to the Prophet Muhammad (pbuh)

Ramadan [ra-ma-daan] – the month of fasting

salah [sal-aa] – the five special Muslim daily prayers

subhah [sub-haa] – a string of beads for counting prayer-phrases, usually 33 or 99

tarawih [tara-wih] – evening prayers said during Ramadan

wudu [woo-doo] – the special wash that is done before praying

Glossary

Allah the name for God in Arabic

Arabic the language of the Qur'an

bazaar a market

chandelier a light holder that hangs from the ceiling

community group of people who have some things in common

fast go without food and drink

Hajj the pilgrimage to Makkah

imam the leader of prayers in a mosque

Islam the Muslim religion founded by the Prophet Muhammad (pbuh)

khutbah a short talk or sermon

madrasah the mosque school, where people can learn more about Islam

minaret a tower on a mosque. It is often used to make the call to prayer.

niche a hollow space in a wall

pilgrim someone who makes a special religious journey

pilgrimage a religious journey to a holy place

pbuh Muslims always write "pbuh" whenever they mention the Prophet Muhammad. It means "Peace be upon him".

prophet someone sent by God with messages for people

Qur'an the collection of messages given to the Prophet Muhammad (pbuh)

Ramadan the month of fasting

salah the five special Muslim daily prayers

shrine a very holy place, where people go to worship

worship to show respect and love for God

wudu the special wash that is done before praying

Finding out more

Visiting a mosque

The best way to arrange a visit to a local mosque is to contact the imam and set up a date and time. Most imams regard such visits as part of their work, but mosques are busy places so it is always best to arrange something in advance.

When at the mosque, visitors should behave quietly and politely. They should wear clothes that will allow them to sit comfortably on the floor. Women and girls should not wear short skirts, but longer skirts and trousers are fine. It is polite for women and girls to take a scarf to cover their heads. Visitors should also take off their shoes before going inside.

More books to read

Celebrations: Ramadan and Id Ul-Fitr, Mandy Ross (Heinemann Library, 2001)

Holy Places: Makkah, Mandy Ross (Heinemann Library, 2002)

Religions of the World: Islam, Sue Penney (Heinemann Library, 2002)

Useful websites

www.bbc.co.uk/religion/religions/islam/
A detailed website containing lots of information about Islam and the Muslim way of life.

www.ngfl.ac.uk/re/hanfia1.htm
This website provides a tour of the Hanfia Mosque in Bradford, in the United Kingdom.

Disclaimer
All the Internet addresses (URLs) given in this book were valid at the time of going to press. However, due to the dynamic nature of the Internet, some addresses may have changed, or sites may have ceased

Index